ETERNAL SAUDI ARABIA

ETERNAL SAUDI ARABIA

Photographs and Text by

RICK GOLT

ELK PUBLICATIONS London, England

Designed by Adrian Wilson, San Francisco

Composition in Centaur and Palatino types
by Mackenzie-Harris Corp. and
The Press in Tuscany Alley, San Francisco

Printing co-ordination by
Saunders Art & Design Ltd.
Vancouver, B.C.

Photo optical equipment:
Nikon of Japan

Lithographed in Canada

ETERNAL SAUDI ARABIA

Introduction

Saudi Arabia is a land with an incredibly rich heritage, a land of proud and strong people, a land of harsh beauty and immense variety. I travelled in the Kingdom as a photographer and writer with the goal of assembling a book that would portray something of this great beauty and cultural heritage. I hasten to add that this book is in no way intended to be an overall study or evaluation of the modern world of Saudi Arabia. Rather, it is very simply a collection of vignettes, of artistic impressions, thoughts, and experiences that are important to me. It is a study of the grandeur of the desert and mountains, of the sand and rock, that for centuries have provided the forge upon which the Saudi character has been formed. The collection provides glimpses into the lives of a people who have built a culture and heritage. It is a very personal book. This land became a very special place to me. There I found a unique mood and atmosphere: the eternal *spirit* of Saudi Arabia.

In my efforts to express this *spirit*, I often felt that I was trying to photograph more than a physical object. When I photographed the silent stones of a watchtower, I would sense voices talking in excitement at the vision of troops advancing on camels and horses. When the sun settled in glowing splendor and the last traces of the day's heat slipped away, I would feel the warmth of the coffee coals being stirred to flame for the evening in a campsite. I would look at the solid earth and clay bricks of the palaces and fortresses and see robed figures moving along the walls. Beneath the brilliant sun, a figure in the village path would turn and duck into a home, and I would feel the quick fresh cool of the shaded interior. When I saw a shepherd with his flock on a hillside, I felt that I had stood there long ago and listened to the soft whisper of the wind and the gentle munching of the sheep.

Even now I often wonder how it began . . .

I

Well over a year ago, a friend from Saudi Arabia and I sat talking in the shade beside a swimming pool in Hawaii. As a photographer and writer, I was curious to know more of his land that lay half-way around the world. I sat fascinated as he described the many wonders of the Kingdom of Saudi Arabia.

He spoke as an artist, of the magnificence of the silent sunrise in the desert, of the vast open areas, and of the roving tribes that finally had forged together into a modern state. My friend's eyes sparkled as he told me of the ageless spirit of the desert and the fiercely proud history of its nomadic tribes. We talked of camels and palaces, of watchtowers and villages. As he described cold nights in high mountains and fresh, clear springs of the oases, I could only stare in amazement. I had always imagined a vast sand kingdom, dotted with tremendous oil fields, a land of new technology and rapidly growing modern cities. His words stirred my imagination for he spoke of a world of incredible beauty and variety, a world known to only a few. He loved this land, and his enthusiasm was contagious.

At one point he rested his chin on the back of his hand and gazed at me. He said that for many years he felt there was a need for a book that could capture the spirit of his land and people. He agreed that there were many fine books that documented nearly every aspect of the

Kingdom. He knew of no book, however, that justly portrayed the beauty of the land or that demonstrated a full appreciation of this culture and heritage that went beyond history. Within minutes we had agreed that this would be our goal —we would create such a book . . .

With the whine of the aircraft's turbines still ringing in my ears, I descended the ramp into the blinding midday sunlight of Riyadh. Immediately I was engulfed by an endless array of new experience. As a guest of my friend's family, I found myself in my own private universe. Beyond the walls of their comfortable villa was a world filled with wonderful new foods, sights, and

One of the modern buildings in Riyadh

sounds. Almost everything in daily life, from the poetic flow of the Arabic language to the meal times and business hours, was new to me. Each evening before dinner I would sit in the living room with a gathering of new friends and talk of the Kingdom. Slowly, I became aware of how little I actually knew of this incredible land. Indeed, to my pleasure, very few places on earth have offered such a gratifying surprise as did Saudi Arabia when more of its vast variety and proud character unfolded itself before me. It was unique.

During my first week in Riyadh, I photographed throughout the city: in the *souks* at night, in the castles and streets by day. I made images of beautiful new architecture, of jet contrails curving silently across a sunset sky into the majestic silhouette of the water tower. All the sights and sounds were new—a rush of activity in a new world, a world that was moving hurriedly to a position of international prominence. It was almost too much to comprehend. Wherever I would point my camera, there would be still another facet of this new-found kaleidoscope of activity. I could only pause in confusion and try to make a unity out of the myriad parts. Amid the honking of horns in the traffic of a modern and growing metropolis, I would walk in the cool night past the giant cranes that work around the clock, their dazzling floodlights illuminating the core of yet another new building. Inside this same rush of

Watertower, Riyadh

13

Qasr, Riyadh

Qasr, Riyadh

activity, a great serenity came to me when I heard the evening call to prayer from the nearby mosques—a beautiful and musical chant that floated across the air beneath the rapidly-darkening orange sky. It simply overwhelmed me!

In my everyday life I was suddenly granted a new form of objectivity. Rather than learning from books, I was by circumstance freed to measure what I saw and experienced, and to express it in my own visual medium—photography. Because I could neither read nor understand Arabic, I was almost totally dependent upon my own senses, free to draw my own visual interpretations from the environment itself, free to work and create. Like a child I was able only to see and react, rather than to understand and evaluate.

Woodcutter beside river, near Az Zafir

In my wanderings through Riyadh I found myself drawn more and more to the great palaces and fortresses. Their massive walls held a pride and dignity that seemed to symbolize an eternal spirit. They represented all the strength and character I found in this energetic nation; yet, in their shaded courtyards and splashing fountains, I found a beauty and peace that told of the sensitivity, hospitality, and kindness that I found in the Saudi people. As I shook the weathered but gentle hand of the gatekeeper at the Murabba Palace and bid him good-bye, I knew that I had found what I felt represented the beauty and heritage of Saudi Arabia.

I knew I would have to pursue that beauty and heritage, and capture it. I had to get into the desert and mountains, the villages and farms in the far-reaching corners of the land. I would have to explore and probe until I came to know more of these proud people who had swept back and forth across the endless sands in battles that transformed warring tribes into a mighty kingdom. I had to see for myself the sites of these legendary battles, to climb the stone steps in Rashid's fortress and stare across the glittering sands from which Abdul Aziz brought his troops. With my own eyes I had to survey the surrounding desert from the watchtower that looked down on hundreds of flat, empty miles, across which any attacker had to pass. I had to feel the blazing sun on my head and back, to study the mirage, floating on

Al-Musmak Fortress, Riyadh

Castle and Village, south of Abha

Qasr Al-Murabba, Riyadh

Qasr Al-Murabba, Riyadh

shimmering air above the sand and stone, and to try to comprehend the heritage of the Saudi. I had to gain some understanding of this vast land of sudden storms, ringing heat and freezing nights, and to pry loose its meanings and express them in words and photographs. The quotation: "A society's greatest promise lies in the ability to harness modern technology to the wisdom of its cultural heritage" formed the central theme that was to help unify the myriad different worlds of Saudi Arabia I found in my work . . .

It suddenly struck me: the project was a reality—but I had no "party," could speak only a few words of Arabic, and knew very little of the Kingdom that lay

beyond the gates of Riyadh. Thoughts tumbled through my mind as I hurried back to my friend's villa.

Here again, fortune was kind to me. I had no more than mentioned my concern to my friend than the familiar twinkle began to dance in his eyes. In fact he beamed a broad smile and said that he had an associate that he felt could be of great assistance to me. Without hesitation, he turned to leave, calling over his shoulder to have some tea and that he would be right back. In less than ten minutes my friend reappeared in the doorway with a rather short man in a brown suit, whom he promptly introduced as "Kamal."

18

Kamal was quite pleasant and polite, and seemed eager to hear of our project. He had spent much of his earlier career in the Forestry Department. It rapidly became obvious that he not only knew the Kingdom extremely well but was a source of knowledge on the peoples and history of the various areas. More important, he knew the roads, the villages and towns, the oases and the desert. Almost before I finished outlining my ambitious plan, Kamal declared he was ready to leave on this incredible journey. He was immensely enthusiastic about the project, and even more excited about travelling throughout the endless open spaces of the Kingdom he loved so well. He was like a child with a new toy, a surprise gift.

Immediately, we spread the maps on the dining room table to begin preparing an itinerary. Kamal hung his jacket on the back of a chair, lit a cigarette, and sat down with a pad of yellow paper. With quick, deft strokes he listed in Arabic each item we felt we might need, the type of vehicle and special equipment. With these lists we began an undertaking far more fascinating and involved than I ever could have imagined. I began a period of several of the most interesting months of my life and a journey that was to take me over five thousand miles into a world that few are ever privileged to see or know. . .

Gate, Qasr Al-Murabba, Riyadh

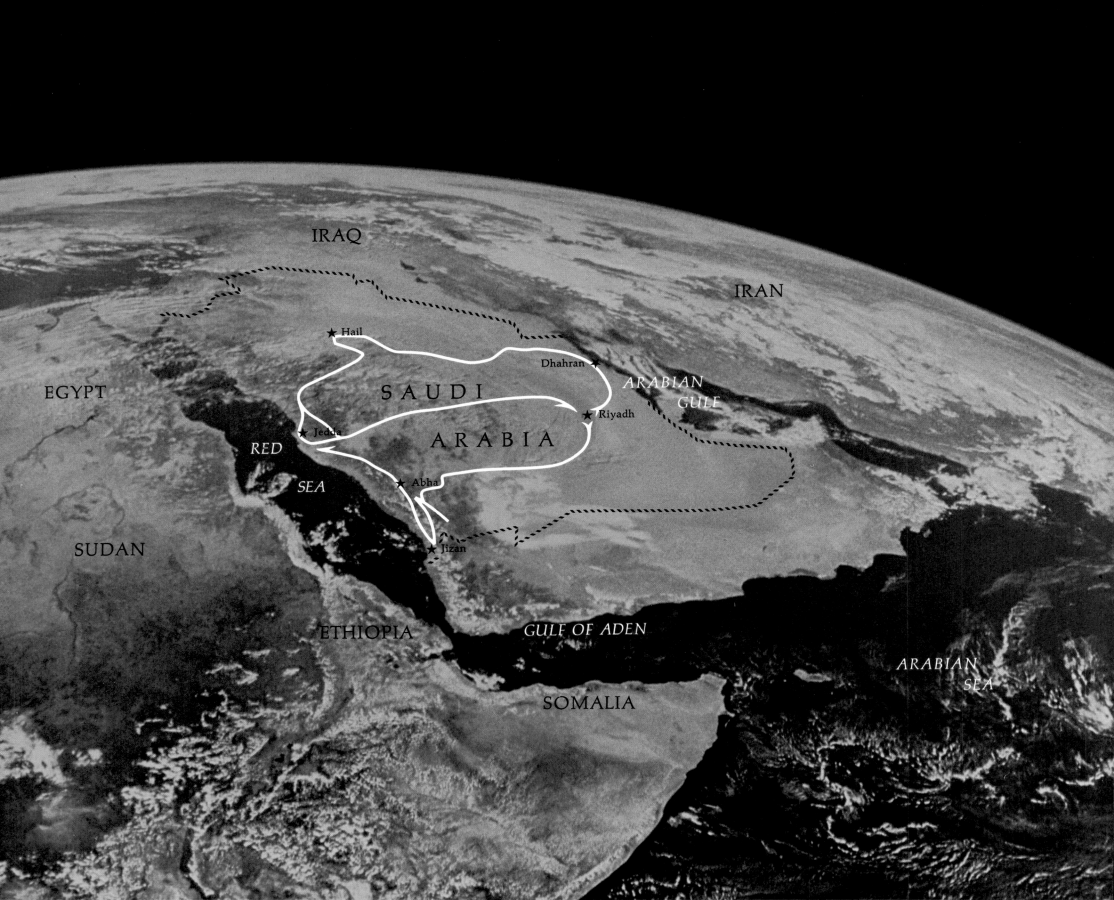

To explore the length and breadth of Saudi Arabia is a staggering idea: it is not an undertaking to be considered lightly. The immense area of the Kingdom stuns the mind—thirteen hundred miles long and eight hundred miles wide, it is larger than most of western Europe! I spent hours studying our route on the best maps I could find. Gradually I developed an appreciation that the lonely dots of cities and towns were hundreds of miles apart. As my eyes skimmed across the magic names, hundreds of miles turned into thousands. The distances alone left me a little light-headed. Something on one map struck me as unique: some areas had no roads, no names, no towns. One area was labelled simply: *Rub Al Khali*, ''The Empty Quarter.'' On the map it is a giant void, a blank area of paper larger than California or France that fills the entire southeast quadrant of the Kingdom!

Our route was a giant circle around the Kingdom. On the first tour, we would go east to the Gulf, through Hofuf and the Al Hasa oasis area, then north to the coastal fishing towns. Next, we would parallel the Trans-Arabian Pipeline, north and inland, through the deserts of the most renowned Bedouin tribes—the Shammar, the Mutayr, names from a powerful history. From some point on that road, we would select a route west to Buraydah and Hail, then southwest to Medina and the trade routes south to Jedda.

At the end of this tour, we would break, replenish, organize and then apply what we'd learned to the second giant half-circle. This second tour would take us east and south, through Al Kharj and Al Aflaj to the southern deserts. From Wadi Al Dawasir, we would cross open desert beside the Empty Quarter to Abha, and then branch down to Najran and Jizan on the Red Sea, and finally move north to Jedda, completing the circle and crossing the Kingdom.

Our camel for this caravan was ''Jimmy,'' a giant GMC wagon. Seemingly built of forged iron, the Jimmy is a favored vehicle in the Kingdom; and later its great

Fishing Boat Sculpture, Corniche, Jedda

capacity and strong pulling power proved more valuable than its bulk and weight. Without its cavernous rear compartment, we often would have had no place to sleep; and without its massive tires we might well have stayed up to our axles in the soft sand of many *wadis*. Although Jimmy is a relatively new creature to the desert, he has adapted quite well. He was to prove ideal for our needs not only as a vehicle but often as a house and restaurant.

If there is anything that seemed more appealing than being in the open desert it was being in the open desert with a good supply of food and water. After having provisioned our four-wheel camel with boxes of canned food, five cases of Sohat mineral water, pots, pans, blankets and spare parts, he sagged low on his rear springs. When we'd loaded the basic equipment through the back doors, there was scarcely space for cameras and personal gear; but in the desert it seemed wiser to take what we might need than to later wish we had it . . .

At last everything was ready. My friend and I stood in the darkened courtyard listening to the splashing of the fountain. In the morning Kamal would pick me up at dawn —less than nine hours, I thought, as we watched the evening stars grow brighter. We bid each other good-bye, and after I watched my friend disappear through the lighted doorway into the villa, I went to my room. The great adventure was about to begin . . .

Apartment complex, Jedda

Boy releasing pigeon, Buraydah

II

Thoughts turning in my mind, I spent a restless night reviewing our supplies, getting up to check the shutters on each camera and sealing them back in their aluminum cases. If I had forgotten anything it wasn't because I didn't consider it that night. I slept only three hours. When I woke, the sky was black, and in the breathless air all was silent, except for a dog barking somewhere far across the slumbering city. No one but me, the dog, and the giant crane operators were awake. It was a good feeling. I showered quickly and dressed in what I considered to be my desert outfit.

Seldom can I recall feeling greater excitement for the unknown than when I carried my carefully-packed cases to the gate in the crisp dawn air. I set them on the pavement and looked around the tiny garden in the dark, feeling rather out of place. I turned and went back into the house to once again trace over our route on my small map. On this map, all seemed deceptively simple. The handful of towns appeared reassuringly close together. I knew too well the thousands of miles of the route, not to mention the side explorations we anticipated. We had no daily itinerary. My plan was simply to follow this route, diverting occasionally, and stopping to explore and photograph everything of interest. Since I had very little knowledge of what lay ahead, I could plan in only the most general sense. I knew that everything would take longer than anyone suspected, for I alone

knew the many long hours I would spend creating the photography.

I drew a deep breath, folded the map, switched off the lamp, and went outside to await Jimmy and my companions. Although Jedda lay only six hundred miles to the West, we would travel through a great northeasterly circle to reach it. Our route would take us nearly three thousand miles, I thought, as I saw the headlights of the vehicle stabbing their way along the walls of the street. The sky was turning a pale gray.

Our third member arrived within a few minutes. Kamal's friend, Murieed, a Saudi in his early twenties, adjusted his *ghotra* after straightening himself from his father's sedan. Murieed and his father embraced and stood talking across the street for several minutes, while Kamal and I loaded the cameras into the remaining corners of Jimmy. The sedan pulled away. Murieed tucked a case under one arm and a blanket roll under the other and started across the street with a grin on his face. It seemed he also realized that through some quirk of fate we were about to embark on an extraordinary adventure.

In the hazy dawn we shook hands and introduced ourselves. After stowing the last bits of luggage, we made the first photographs. Taking turns with a camera, we each photographed the other two posing proudly beside Jimmy, who was clean and polished, ready for the road. The early traffic was already honking its way along the adjacent main street, so we settled into the truck and started the engine.

The traffic was still fairly light, and we moved along in it through the streets of downtown Riyadh. The city was waking rapidly: shops throwing open their shutters, men washing taxis, trucks delivering everything imaginable to the endless shops, children carrying their leather bags to school. A morning breeze picked up and the air was fresh and cool. Even though we were still driving on familiar streets, an immense wave of relief swept through me. At last we were underway!

Riyadh ended abruptly. Within a space of a hundred yards, there was no longer a city. I turned my head. Buildings, houses, and fences grew rapidly smaller in the distance. Like walking through a door, we had struck out into the desert. It was a clean break. Ahead, all the eye could see was flat shale, stone, and sand. Not a house or building dotted the land, not a pole or fence; only a disappearing triangle of black asphalt lay beneath us. The sky and sand curved ahead endlessly.

Now my doubts were gone. We were setting off to discover Saudi Arabia. My apprehensions faded into a feeling of great exhilaration. Kamal was laughing and seemed almost on the verge of song. He was delighted to be out in the open country again. Above the rush of the wind Murieed and I talked about the work that I intended to do. It was as difficult to explain then as it was when I began to develop the great plan. Of one thing he was certain: even if I was crazy, I was overjoyed with the desert.

Frequently I had Kamal stop so I could walk onto the sand and make a few photographs —of what, I later found, was some of the less interesting terrain in the Kingdom. But each time I would climb back into the seat, Kamal would smile and ask if I had "gotten some nice pictures." For the first hundred miles or so we rode along, getting acquainted with each other, with the project, with the desert.

Jimmy, Ad Dahna

We approached a darkening sky that appeared to hold a light rain. The road ahead grew hazy and blurred. Swiftly we moved into it. First, a gust of wind. All around us the air swirled gray-brown. "Sand," Kamal muttered, rolling up his window. We slowed the truck. Visibility was down to about a hundred yards. Great sheets and tails of sand washed across the road and stung the windshield. Ever-shifting patterns slid across the black asphalt. Then, abruptly, we broke out into blue sky again. It was only a passing breath of wind, not a true sandstorm; it was merely a mass of dry air playing with the powder-like grains of the desert, spinning them into the sky. The shower fell briefly, and then it was gone.

We stopped at the side of the road. Midmorning: it was tea time, a ritual we would follow each day. We pulled out the thermos of hot tea and sat in the shade of our "camel," the only shade for miles and miles. After one quick glass of tea, I picked up a camera bag and started into the sand.

I crunched my way along level sand and over several slight ridges. In a few minutes the sparkle of Jimmy was a bright dot in a vast ocean of empty sand. Around me the gradual roll of the sand sparkled with winking lights. It was amazingly clean, like water. The hot, dry air burned down on my head and into my eyes. A light wind kept the surface sand in motion, pushing the finest grains along the desert floor, making it difficult to focus the eye or camera. At the top of a ridge, the sand sped up and stung my ankles through my trousers. As I descended the ridge, the endless pressure of sand moved up to knee level, and the sand underfoot became soft and deep.

I stopped on a ridge. I was alone. My own universe! The sun and sky above me; the sand below, its surface washing along like a fog in the gentle, hot wind. The only sound was the soft hiss of the sliding surface of the desert. I knelt and put my hand slowly into this moving, almost invisible stream of sand. As my fingers touched the floor of the desert, the tingling flow of sand reached only my wrist. A strangely pleasant stream of air and sand.

As I straightened, I turned and gazed across the dunes. I felt strangely at home in this vast expanse. There was a feeling of relief and freedom that I could never explain. It was the beginning of a long series of things which I would find difficult to explain.

As I started back to the vehicle, I turned several times, certain I had heard a voice, a sound; but there was only the hiss of the shifting sand. I was convinced there was something else. I was determined to find it . . .

Blowing sand, near Khurais

III

On our first afternoon I finally saw one. We were crossing a wide area of sand dunes, and there he was far off across the sand. After miles and miles of empty desert, the camel seemed almost an apparition. We stopped the truck, and when the engine died we were instantly engulfed in the silent, soft wind of the desert.

I squinted across the glare of the sand, and there amidst the millions of needles of light stood a real, live camel. He was not like the camels in books or zoos. This was no strange and awkward creature. Here was the camel that had dwelled in the deserts for countless centuries. Watching him brought the trance-like feeling of staring into a campfire. Alone on the sand of his desert, this camel seemed the most graceful and free of creatures. Even though he was at some distance, I could almost feel the fluid flow of his legs as he slowly and carefully coasted forward on the sand, stopping, turning, and lowering his long neck to graze.

As though compelled by an unseen gesture, I pulled the camera bag from the car and started toward the camel. I kept my eyes fixed on his undulating path across the dunes, and dragged my feet ahead —less gracefully than he —in pursuit. Even with the light breeze, the shimmering heat folded over me. The heat of the sand came rapidly through my shoes, and the closeness of the hot air rose and fell with the slightest change of the breeze.

When I crested a small dune and descended into a shallow bowl of sand, the breeze fell and the heat pressed instantly into my back and face. Tiny beads of perspiration formed, only to chill and vanish the instant I emerged back into the moving air again.

My camel was obviously far more comfortable out there than I, for he continued to amble casually along at a right angle to the path I had chosen to intercept him. I drew within a hundred yards or so and stopped. Breathing heavily from the walk through the hot sand, I watched in amazement as the camel continued along his path in a gentle swaying walk. He would place each large pad of

a foot carefully on the sand and roll forward into another step. His huge foot seemed like a large skin of water that spread out onto the sand to make a soft bed from which his long legs could pivot.

Breathing deeply to slow my pounding heart, I carefully took out a camera and made several photographs of my first camel. Then I hurried ahead of him to make further studies. Throughout all this, my camel was completely cooperative, as he was oblivious to my motions. If he was aware of my presence, nothing about his disdainful

attitude gave any indication of it. After walking almost at his side and trying to hear even the slightest sound from his padded, silent feet, I finally decided to stop. Without a break in his casual pace, my camel continued away from me and down a gentle slope.

He seemed almost a part of the desert itself, gracefully floating across its surface, moving further from where I stood on the rise. As I watched, I slowly realized that he was not alone. On the ridges, large groups of his brothers and sisters, mere dots on the sand horizon, nodded slowly as they fed. As I studied the desert carefully, I realized that there were hundreds of them, all grazing peacefully there in the pounding heat, completely at ease. My camel was moving patiently toward them.

Slowly, I began to realize that I was very hot and that the breeze had fallen. It was time to return to the truck. The truck? With a quickening pulse, I looked all around for the truck but saw only sand. No sign of the road. It wasn't possible! I couldn't have come more than a half-mile. I could now see camels everywhere, on all sides of me, but I couldn't catch a glimpse of the truck. I put the camera into the bag, feeling the intense heat of its steel body.

Near Ghawar

Az Zilfi

My mind told me that I was in no danger. Yet I was feeling the heat more every minute and something began to gnaw inside me. I frowned. The truck had to be less than ten minutes away —a ten-minute walk at the furthest. Simple logic. At the truck were friends, food and water. If I didn't return soon, surely they would begin to worry and then look for me. I was certain they had seen the direction I had taken . . .

I looked down at my footprints. With a stupid grin, I began to walk back along the depressions my feet had left in the sand. Pausing for breath, I continued methodically to follow my own tracks. However, as I came to the ridge of a dune, the frown returned. Where were my footprints? My pulse rose again, and the heat seemed suddenly more intense. There seemed to be footprints everywhere, and at the same time there were no footprints at all. I glanced around hurriedly. Where were the camels?

Suddenly, a friend's light-hearted comment in Riyadh rang in my ears: "Just stick with the car. You'll never get lost —might be covered over with sand, but you'll not get lost."

I wasn't lost. Nonsense. I wasn't going to get lost. I had to be within a few minutes of the highway. I started climbing up the ridgeline. From its summit I would be able to survey the entire area. With fierce determination, I slugged up the ridge in the deep sand that began to fill my shoes.

At the top, I took a deep breath and searched for the highway. To my confusion, nothing but rolling dunes lay endlessly ahead. There *was* no road. Yet surely I would see it from here. I had to.

Suddenly a horn broke the silence! The road. Of course it was the road. The horn had to come from a car on the road. My eyes strained against the dazzling light. I could see nothing.

Again, the horn. Three long tones. They seemed to come from behind me and far away. I turned and with my eyes squinted I made out the black band of a highway behind and below me. It had to be the road. It couldn't possibly be any other road —there was no other road. But how was it behind me?

Beside the stripe of asphalt, I could barely discern a blue speck. Jimmy. I could scarcely believe my eyes. It seemed miles away and much further below me than it should have been. Yet there it was. Unmistakably.

It took me nearly thirty minutes to slog my way back over the dunes to the road. I found my two friends sitting beside the truck in a sliver of shade, drinking tea as I approached. I swung the camera bag back onto the seat. Kamal asked if I had gotten some good pictures. I nodded my head and mumbled that I had . . . and slumped down beside them and drank half a liter of mineral water in one continuous gulp.

Kamal smiled and handed me a cup of tea. "Tell me when you want to go far from the truck again," he said, tapping the cap back on the thermos. "One of us can come with you to help carry things." I agreed that that would be helpful, and would also allow me to take the tripod. But I understood what he meant, and felt a little foolish —and more than a little lucky.

IV

We had driven to the old city of Diriyah for the afternoon to explore and photograph. Less than twenty minutes from the rush of downtown Riyadh, this legendary town is a treasury of Saudi heritage. Here was a town of great history and tradition, a town I felt I must explore.

Throughout the village were many abandoned wells. These were built of fitted stones, which formed the shaft into the earth. On the surface stood the rock walls of the well topped with a palm log. Years ago, long ropes were slung over this log to haul water, either by hand or

Restoration, Diriyah

by camels, from the well. When I found the wells, I felt like an archaeologist. Here were ancient structures that had formed the core of village life; upon their water depended the existence and prosperity of the village. The wells were quite intact, and I felt that by studying them closely I could learn much about the role the precious water had played in daily life. I began tracing the channels and spillways, the basins used for storage and for watering animals.

It was with wonderful excitement that I had discovered a tunnel that angled steeply down into one of the main well shafts. Since I could see almost nothing below the first ten feet of the well shaft itself, it seemed important that I descend the side tunnel to explore what great treasures it might reveal.

I handed Murieed everything except one camera and two lenses. Then I began to creep carefully down the dark tunnel, feeling my way with one hand and crouching to avoid the low ceiling. Progress was slow. After several feet, the floor turned to the softest of sand, which apparently had drifted into the tunnel since the last man descended this passage. I thought to myself that there probably were steps beneath the sand which surely would make the trip easier. At each step, I slid several feet further, as the deep sand pushed down ahead of me.

Soon I was crouched low, sweating profusely, and powdered with fine dust and sand. I was coughing and barely able to see. I turned to look back up the angled tube. Kamal was peering into the darkness that contained me.

"Come on back out of there," he shouted. "You'll not find anything down there."

While the dust settled I paused to regain my breath. My heart was pulsing against the sweat-soaked camera tucked under my shirt to protect it from the dust. I had to reach the main well shaft. First it was curiosity, then, the excitement of discovery. Now there was pride mixed with fear. I suppose I wanted to be the first man to descend a well tunnel and photograph its interior. Perhaps I just wanted to see the bottom of the main shaft. My reasons were mixed. But I didn't want to be the man who climbed back up the tunnel just because it was a little dusty and dark.

My teeth gritty with sand, I pressed on deeper.

Suddenly, the earth slid from beneath my feet. The sand floor of the tunnel was slipping down toward the main shaft, pulling me with it!

Diriyah

41

Frantically, I scratched at the earthen walls of the tunnel as they glided past. I flailed my arms against its sides and its ceiling, hoping to grab anything.

Ahead of me appeared a faint gray light. It grew larger as I continued to bump and slide my way along with the sand: the main well shaft! Somehow I had to stop.

Desperately I tried to dig my feet into the sand, but it merely slid me along like a conveyor belt.

I was slipping into the main shaft!

A black hole suddenly opened below me. I was losing my balance. I threw myself backwards into the sliding

sand. By some miracle, my hand grasped something solid. I clutched the object with both hands and held on with all my strength. Sand poured down over me. Scarcely able to breathe, I ducked down and held on fiercely.

Then it ceased.

I heard voices crying and echoing throughout the chamber. The dust was so thick I could see only yellow light overhead. Carefully, I pulled myself toward the wooden beam on which my hands locked. With each motion, small streams of sand spilled into the main shaft. Finally I dragged myself to the beam at the edge of the shaft. I stood up in the sand at the end of the tunnel.

I shuddered. I had almost gone over the edge!

I strained my neck around and looked straight up the shaft to the sky. It appeared almost white from the bottom of the well, and the stone walls became a dark gray as my eyes adjusted to the dim light. I guessed that I was about sixty feet down the shaft, a seemingly bottomless cavern. Above me I saw Kamal and Murieed, who looked like small insects peering over the rim of the well. They were shouting to me, but the echo inside the chamber garbled their words.

Cautiously, I peered down into the main shaft. Blackness. I stood totally still in the musty air. No breeze had

43

ever blown here. The dust was settling slowly. I was still alive, holding onto the beam —and not tumbling down what appeared to be a bottomless pit.

As long as I didn't move, the sand in the steep side tunnel I had descended stayed in place. At the least motion, the sand would begin to slide down around me into the main shaft, threatening to pull me into the well.

After some minutes, the air was again clear. I looked straight up to the sky and watched Murieed and Kamal scurrying around the mouth of the well. I called out that I was all right. Echoes bounced around the stone walls. Taking a deep breath, I finally drew out the camera and held it into the shaft to make several random views of the interior of the well.

Then with all the care I could manage, I hesitantly began to pick my way back up through the sand tunnel, still grasping the beam behind me. The floor of sand slid,

but only slightly. Evidently most of the loose material had gone down the main shaft.

Steadily, I made my way up the tunnel. Several times I had to hold my breath and press my hands against the side walls and watch in horror as the rivers of sand slid around my ankles. Fortune was kind: each river slowed and stopped. At last, with a burst of energy, I plowed my way out of the tunnel.

Sunlight.

Murieed and Kamal were all around me, slapping off the sand and dust and asking if I was all right. There in the heat and light I recovered. I was the only man they knew who had descended into an ancient well —or who was foolish enough to try. With a measured pride, I told them that it had been quite fascinating —exciting. I avoided mentioning that they almost had to send someone down a rope to the bottom of the shaft to find me.

V

In the south of the Kingdom, the sun seems to burn with a greater intensity, probably because there is often less wind there. It burned down with a fury on the three of us when we finally stepped back from our exhausting efforts and accepted the fact that Jimmy was buried in soft sand up to his axles.

We had left Khamsin along a dotted line marked on the map as "New Road Construction" for Khamis Mushayt. The line paralleled the Empty Quarter to the west for nearly three hundred miles, with only one dot along the route: Tathlith. In Khamsin we had heard varied opinions of the road to the south. "Obviously it's a good route," Kamal had said, "because the big lorries use it to bring supplies from the south."

Now we stood in the glaring light looking at the *Ad Dhana* that surrounded us —just as the map had warned. *Ad Dahna*, the regions of soft sand, sounds less perilous than it is. The soft sand can swallow your shoes with each step, and it now threatened to swallow Jimmy. We had followed the "New Construction" across thirty miles of beautiful, flat asphalt until a detour sign directed us off onto hard desert floor. Then for another thirty miles we drove parallel to the raised roadbed, where scrapers and loaders moved like giant beetles surfacing the road. We had passed dozens of huge Mercedes trucks loaded to the brim of their brightly painted side-

boards. Always we held a southwest direction, and always the roadbed stayed on our right flank. We had jounced and banged over smaller rocks and among rough outcroppings of shale, as we made our way toward Tathlith.

Most changes in the desert are slow and subtle. It took me several hours to realize that although we still headed southwest by my Swiss compass, we could no longer trace the fine line of raised roadbed to the west. Large trucks had become fewer each hour. Kamal said most of them left at dawn and were probably past us. The gradual change from hard earth to sand beneath our tires was scarcely perceptible. Kamal occasionally had to swerve to avoid a soft patch of rock and sand; then more and more frequently, he had to power through deeper beds of sand that tugged at the wheels as they strained to gain footing.

Now we were jolted into reality: Jimmy was sunk deep in the sand. Mysteriously, gently rolling and slithering sand appeared around us. Nothing else, nothing at all. It had been at least two hours since we had seen another vehicle. Other tire tracks no longer marked the desert. We were alone.

The peaceful heat of the desert was suddenly a powerful enemy, a threat to our existence. My mind flooded with

stories of sandstorms and unbearable heat I had heard in the city. Scorpions, snakes, and quicksand took on new meanings as I stared across the open furnace of the sand. Out here it was obvious that a man on foot would not survive more than a few miles. I felt quite small in the immensity of the silent heat.

Murieed climbed up on Jimmy's roof and for several minutes silently squinted in each direction. "We must find something to free the wheels," he said simply, and began trudging toward a nearby ridge.

Kamal suggested that we dig the sand out from under the truck. For almost a half hour, we scooped at the mass of sand that surrounded the rear wheels and axle. It was like trying to dig the tires out of an ocean. Our efforts produced only a shallow opening under the truck bed and an appreciation that Jimmy was larger than we realized. The prospect of digging the truck out of the sand bordered on hopeless, I thought as I slouched back into the shade and drank deeply from my plastic water bottle.

I jerked erect at what sounded like thunder falling on the other side of the truck. There stood Murieed, dusting his hands together. At his feet lay an eight-foot-long section of corrugated tin. I could only stare open-

Near Tathlith

Western edge, Rub Al Khali

mouthed at this miracle. Where could he possibly have found such a thing? But then, he found camels I could not see even when he pointed at them.

He began to struggle with the tin. Between the three of us we managed to get it under one of the rear tires, and thereby formed a short ramp on which we hoped to drive the truck out of the hole. Kamal's spirits rose, and he adjusted his cowboy hat onto the back of his head and hopped into the driver's seat.

After several minutes of straining and groaning and spinning a cloud of sand into the air, Jimmy had dug

himself firmly back into the holes. Kamal turned off the engine, got out, and looked angrily at the hot rear tires. A lump continued to rise in my throat, and I could feel the sun stinging the back of my neck. I drank more water, then decided to study our predicament from inside the truck, sheltered from the blinding light. At best, we were in trouble; and I began to feel I was the only one who was fully aware of it.

Kamal walked over, leaned against the door, and took off the hat he always wore when the sun was unusually bright. He wiped his forehead on a shirtsleeve. "Don't worry," he said, quietly. "I see you are worrying, but

you must not. Murieed and I are used to this. It happens all the time. It is always like this driving on the desert tracks—there is no need to worry." He smiled a quiet little smile and nodded his head as if agreeing with himself.

I stared across the sand. I had twice nearly gotten lost on foot within sight of a road; and yet I had calmly watched while we drove ourselves a hundred miles out into empty desert until we got totally stuck in the sand. Idiot! The heat must have affected my mind. How could I have been so stupid?

A shrill hissing of air roused me, and I shook my head and went to the back of the truck. I gasped. My heart leaped back into my throat at the sight of the nearly flat tire. Were they deliberately trying to kill us? "Wait," I called. "You're letting out too much air."

I knew that with less air the tires would flatten and we could get more traction in the deep sand. But with nearly *all* the air out of a tire, we couldn't drive more than a few feet! Already they had most of the air out of the other rear tire, and I felt as flattened as the tires themselves.

The only thing to do now, I thought, was to stay with the truck and hope that another vehicle would spot us. Already I was planning how to spend the last days of my life. How to find rescue. I heard them letting air from the front tires, but could only shake my head. "Terrific," I muttered. "Now maybe we can drive our flat-tired Jimmy out of the sand and cut the tires to ribbons in the first half-mile."

It wasn't easy but somehow on the next attempt at rocking the truck back and forth in his holes, Jimmy struggled and wobbled to his feet on the soft, mushy tires, flapped over the tin roofing, and moved off about twenty yards to solid ground. Kamal turned off the ignition and came dancing out of the truck, laughing and throwing his hat in the air. I managed a faint smile, but didn't share his enthusiasm. We could never drive on those tires. I went back to my water bottle and stared to the south, begging for a glimpse of a vehicle.

Kamal had started the engine again, and it was idling slowly. I gritted my teeth. They're crazy, I thought. Now he was using up the gasoline. I refused to turn around to what I was certain would be the sight of Kamal warming up the engine for the trip, which he did faithfully each morning for at least ten minutes. I simply couldn't watch; but the empty horizon offered no sign of help.

Finally, I could stand it no longer. I spun around. I could hardly believe my eyes. One tire was completely full. Murieed was bending over the rear tire. A small hose

ran from the tire valve and disappeared beneath the opened hood. They had replaced a spark plug with a small pump that was steadily puffing air into the tire. It worked like magic! Kamal commented that *no one* went into the desert without such a pump. Within ten minutes, we had the piece of corrugated tin strapped to the roof and were again bouncing along toward Tathlith. Even though we were moving again and the spirits of my two friends were high, I felt less than comfortable. In the back of my mind loomed the image of miles of open country behind us and the unknown desert before us. It was overwhelming, and for the first time I felt I knew the feeling of being adrift at sea.

More miles, more sand . . .

Again, we plowed to a stop. With only the tin sheeting under the wheels, this time we got out of the sand directly. On and on we went, deeper into the desert. I was growing more uneasy all the time. Even though I had left the driving to Kamal, who had made "this sort of trip" many times, two facts hammered at my brain: we were almost down to a quarter-tank of gas, and we should already be in Tathlith if the map's scale was accurate.

At least now we occasionally saw the tracks of a vehicle in the sand. I asked Kamal to stop. I wanted to discuss our predicament while we still had a few odds on our side.

We drove to a slight rise in a rocky area and stopped. We seemed to be back on one of the tracks, even though it might have been weeks since any vehicles had passed. We still had a quarter-tank of gas and plenty of food and water. I had not the slightest idea of where we were. I asked Kamal where we could find gas.

"The only gas is in Tathlith," he said with irony in his voice, as if this was an obvious fact.

"Then we *must* find it?" I asked skeptically.

"We won't miss it," Kamal said proudly. He looked over at my battered map and tapped the route I'd marked. "You see, as long as we follow your road and your compass, we have to reach Tathlith," he said with incredible innocence.

I slid down in the seat and stared at the simple map. "Are you saying that we won't miss Tathlith because of this map?" I asked hesitantly. . . "Of course," he smiled, and looked straight ahead through the windshield, his hands on the steering wheel, ready to drive.

I felt as though he had hit me with a brick. Somehow without any corroboration we had come all this way through open desert, and he had been relying on *my* map and *my* compass. I licked my dry lips and took a long drink of water. I noticed that I had finished three litres. "Kamal . . ." I began, but I just couldn't say the words. I hadn't been navigating —I'd merely been trying to keep a check on our direction. All I knew was that we had been driving southwest. If we were off course, we could easily have passed Tathlith and never seen it!

The lump welled back in my throat, and I felt a bit light-headed. I started to explain to Kamal where I thought we were but wound up saying that I thought he knew the route to Tathlith. After all, it was *he* who had travelled throughout the Kingdom, not me. The last thread of confidence disappeared, however, when Kamal turned to me and simply said: "But you see, I've never actually travelled in this area. I've never been south of Sulayyil."

I folded my hands on top of my head and tried to think. The fact that we had come one hundred and eighty miles, had only a quarter-tank of gas, and were in the middle of a completely empty desert was now unimportant.

It didn't matter, really. Not now. Nothing mattered except that we find Tathlith.

Again I ticked off logistics in my mind: gasoline, distance, time, food and water —and Tathlith. At least we weren't stuck in the sand. But our options were clear: we couldn't turn back; we had to find the village. Or some-one had to find us.

We discussed the possibilities. Generally, we agreed that Tathlith was probably to the east, and Murieed felt that it was still ahead of us. I had no particular "feeling" for where it was. In fact, I felt rather numb. I had visions of sitting on a rocky knoll as our food and water ran out; but I didn't want to drive aimlessly around the desert. So we sat and talked.

Finally, Kamal looked me intently in the eye and asked: "What is your decision?"

"My decision about what?" I stammered.

"Your decision of which way to go. Shall we continue?" he asked with a smile.

Why was this suddenly my decision?

"Let me think," I said, now totally confused. I got out of the car and walked along a ridge of rock. I saw nothing, and sat down to watch the heat shimmer on the desert.

When I finally returned, I had a plan. "We'll drive another ten miles southwest," I said, with all the con-viction I could manage. "If we don't find more tracks or signs of Tathlith, we'll stop for the night. Maybe we'll see the lights of the village or a vehicle. Maybe we'll see something. If we don't we'll camp there for several days and pray that someone spots us," I said hopefully.

I had a further plan to then drive another ten miles east and wait several more days. That seemed like such a desperate recourse that I didn't want to think of it.

Kamal smiled again: "Then you wish to drive another ten miles on this route?" he asked cheerfully.

"Yes."

As if we were leaving the villa in Riyadh, Kamal started the engine and put the truck into gear. We eased our way down the gradual slope and up the next. I glanced at the odometer. Almost a mile. Then a mile and a half.

Murieed suddenly burst out with a laugh and pounded on the back of my seat. He had been silent for so long that I jumped. "Look . . . look up there," he said, clapping his hands like a child.

To my exhilaration, a dark dot on the next crest turned into a huge truck, painted every color of the rainbow. The driver had spread a mat in the shade beside the truck. He was still asleep when we pulled up. Never in my life had I been so glad to see anyone. Never. We all hurried out of the truck and over to the man, who was rubbing his eyes in astonishment.

We talked for some time. He gave us cans of ice-cold fruit nectar and we gave him bananas and biscuits. He pointed to the left: "Tathlith," he said. Sure enough, I could barely make out the outline of the water tower on a hill.

VI

We turned off the road west of Al Qaysumah, and drove over pavement-smooth stones for several hundred yards and parked Jimmy for the night. Hurriedly, we rearranged our equipment so we could sleep, and ate a light snack. Sitting behind the truck, we watched the last glow of blue and red fade as the light left the sky and the evening chill crept over the desert. It had been a long day, so with scarcely a word we crawled into our blankets.

The dawn was a cool gray haze. I stretched my arms, and somehow managed to roll out the back door of the truck and pull on my clothes. For added warmth, I put on a leather coat and jogged in place. Even though the sun was up, everything was bathed in a soft diffused light. The heavy haze seemed only to increase the cold. I walked some distance from the truck and looked around in awe at the vastness of the Kingdom. As far as the eye could see, dark pebbles and rocks lay on the flat desert floor.

Now Kamal and Murieed were awake, and we prepared a breakfast of tinned foods, biscuits, and some hot coffee. The day grew brighter as the haze burned off, exposing still broader expanses of emptiness. We gathered our gear and repacked the truck. As we warmed the engine, I noticed the dark shapes to the west. They appeared out of place in this area of flat shale and stone, and I decided to investigate.

Distances in the desert are deceiving. After we drove less than a half-mile, I had Kamal stop. There in the thinning haze lay several flat-sided tents of a group of *Badu*, or Bedouin, the legendary nomadic peoples of the desert.

I walked ahead of the truck and stood before the silent forms. All night we had been camped within a mile of each other. I wondered if they had known we were there. It would have been almost impossible for us to have seen them against the sunset.

A nervous excitement rushed through me. These were the people who, for literally thousands of years, roamed the deserts, were always moving, always finding an elusive harmony with the harsh desert world, adapting and adjusting somehow to its demands. Now their world lay before my eyes. As I gazed at the black tents, the Earth seemed to take on a timeless dimension.

I had heard and read much of the noble and simple lives of the *Badu*, and somehow I felt quite naked as I stood there watching for any sign of life. I was apprehensive. My mind was spinning with tales of the fierce camp

dogs, rigid traditions, and proud independence of the *Badu*. These hulking black tents seemed a key to understanding an ancient heritage. I simply stared at them, waiting nervously to see what might happen.

The sun now burned through a blue sky, and the air warmed within a matter of minutes. Finally, several men appeared in front of the tents. One of them strode toward us directly, and we shook hands in greeting. His eyes sparkled but his weathered face seemed cautious and stern. Nothing around me was familiar. I was listening to words I could not understand, words spoken in a desert hundreds of miles from a city that was halfway around the globe. I felt quite alone . . .

After some conversation, the man invited us for *gahwa*, the strong Arabic coffee. We ducked under the heavy black roof of the tent and settled onto woven floor mats. Once out of the sun, we were engulfed by the cooling shade of the heavy goathair tent. The very dry air combined with a slight breeze to make the inside of the tent most pleasant. The tent was open front and rear to the air; and it was very comfortable to relax against the padded leather bag one of the men offered.

Immediately they began the *gahwa* ceremony. It involves no true ritualism as the tea ceremony in Japan does, but it is every bit as traditional and an integral part of everyday life. A young man named Ahmad went outside the rear flap of the tent and began breaking small dry twigs from a branch. He piled these carefully into a pyramid on the smoldering coals of the fire. Near the fire, he placed a brass mortar and pestle and several cloth bags. From these he poured a measure of coffee beans and cardamom seeds, and began methodically to pound and grind them into powder with an even rhythm. He worked with such grace and proficiency that I could not follow his exact technique. While he crushed the beans, a blackened metal pot was heating over the small, blazing fire. The water and the powder were ready at the same time. He put the powder into the *Ib Reek*, the tall brass-spouted coffee pourer, and filled it with steaming water.

After handing the traditional tiny cups around to all of us seated at the mat, he took our cups in the order dictated by custom and poured the amber black liquid from a height of at least a foot, without spilling a drop. Ahmad poured with nonchalance and perfection for each and every cup. After placing the pourer back against the coals, he took a seat in the group.

West of Al Ghayl

I asked Murieed to thank them for their hospitality. They only nodded and said it was their honor that we had come to visit them. Each time a cup was empty, Ahmad would instantly rise and refill it. This continued for some time while we talked. We talked of the desert, the rains of last week, the grass for their goats, and all the details of everyday desert life. They, in turn, were fascinated with our project and seemed eager to help in any way they could. The aroma of coffee was quite pungent; and there in the cool of the tent I found myself growing sleepy as I listened to the musical harmonies of spoken Arabic.

Before our new friend could again refill my cup, I quickly gave it a little shake while handing it to him, signifying that I had had enough. We asked if I could photograph the tents, and if they would permit me to photograph them. As usually was the case, they seemed quite flattered—if a bit puzzled. However, they asked, that I not photograph the women or go near their tent.

Ahmad led me outside. In our halting Arabic-English, he introduced me to a boy who was mending one of the tents, and left us together so I could photograph. Therein began one of the strangest communications I have ever experienced. The boy spoke no English and I, almost no Arabic, so we simply tried to talk our own languages at each other. I explained that I wanted

to photograph the rolling black mountains of the tent roof. He nodded with a big grin at my gestures and answered something in Arabic. I made a number of photographs of the roof, and then did some of him at work on the tent. At first, I thought he was mending a seam; actually, he was attaching a lighter fabric side panel to the woven black roof. He used a method that appeared a combination of sewing and knot tying, using a strong cord for thread.

I asked somewhat uncertainly what he was doing. He nodded at the cord and began to explain in gestures and words. He pulled at the lower tent panel, then pushed against it with his hands, as though he was going to fasten it to the sand. Gradually, to my enlightenment, I could see that he was trying to show me that the heavy roof of the tent was its main strength member. The panel that he was attaching was to direct currents of air inside the tent for cooling. Other panels of heavier cloth were attached to separate sections of the tent to provide protection from strong winds or storms. I watched him move his arms back and forth as though he were the wind itself, pointing first to the roof, the walls, then to the sun and sky. I began to recognize the *Badu* tent as a simple yet highly sophisticated modular shelter.

I thanked the boy and went back through the open end of the tent. I joined the other men, and they welcomed

me to photograph them. I moved around within the tent, photographing them from various angles as they rested and talked through the hottest portion of the day. I told Kamal what I had learned from the boy; Kamal in turn relayed this to our hosts. During what seemed an extremely long discussion, I became uneasy. Our hosts were no longer smiling and their flashing eyes now focused upon Kamal. They glanced questioningly at my cameras and pointed at the floor of the tent with their fingers. I shifted the two cameras to point away from them and drew back as their voices rose.

I now became aware that each of the Badu wore a large, ornate knife in his belt. One of the older men now rested his hand on the dagger as he talked. Had I somehow insulted them? I'd carefully avoided the women's tent. Kamal was gesturing with an upturned hand, as though he were helpless and innocent of whatever was in question.

I shifted uncomfortably and glanced at Kamal. "Is anything wrong?" I squeezed into the rapid exchange of words. He gestured with the side of his hand to wait. This was anything but comforting, and I avoided the glances of our hosts as they continued to talk excitedly.

The voices stopped. Each man fixed his eyes on me. Kamal turned to me and said: "They have asked me how you know so much of their tent if you cannot truly speak Arabic? They think you are trying to make fun of them, that you really do speak Arabic."

The eyes watched me unblinkingly, and somehow

the daggers at their belts seemed more conspicuous than they had earlier. I swallowed hard and leaned toward Kamal. "You know I can't speak Arabic," I replied angrily.

"Yes, but *they* don't."

I turned to the elder men and said in English that the boy had only tried to explain to me about the tent in Arabic, and that I really didn't know very much about the tent and truly didn't understand Arabic. I realized how silly I must have sounded.

Kamal broke in and spoke over my voice, but the men's eyes were watching me sternly. Kamal gestured and sounded as though he were pleading for my life. I grew increasingly aware of how removed from my world we actually were . . .

One of the men put down his coffee cup and clapped his hands on the sand. Suddenly everyone in the tent broke into uproarious laughter. I sat puzzled now by the bright eyes and laughter. Ahmad came over and offered me a fresh cup of coffee, laughing as he poured. Murieed was the first to break the spell. "It's a little joke," he grinned. "When you were outside, they said you seemed so serious that they wanted to play a little trick on you. Surely you weren't frightened?"

"No," I said slowly, again eyeing the daggers and thinking of the long history of desert warfare. In embarrassment, I returned to my cameras and made some more studies of the interior of the tent and the men, who were still laughing and drinking coffee.

Ahmad prepared more coffee along with a bowl of dates. I sat through a few cups of coffee, then said that I thought we should leave. The afternoon was passing rapidly, and I knew that soon the men must return to the flock. Kamal smiled and said that they wanted us to stay the night with them.

67

"We can't do that," I said, surprised that he hadn't mentioned it earlier.

"Why not?" he asked.

"We really should keep moving," I said, thinking of the thousands of miles we planned to cover. My two companions nodded. And after many formal goodbyes and thanks, we finally lumbered away in Jimmy toward Az Zilfi.

We rode in silence, and I was alone with my thoughts. I had enjoyed the visit with the hospitable *Badu* but I was somewhat uncomfortable. I would have liked to stay. I felt that I would have learned far more if we *had* stayed the night with them. Yet something told me that I should press onward to discover more of this incredible land.

As I watched the darkening desert slip past the window of the car, I marvelled at the life of the *Badu*. It is a life I had never known or imagined — almost unique in today's world. He lives his own life on his own terms, with little interaction with anyone else. His world is the solitude of the desert, the endless search for grass for the herd, and a simple unity with nature. Somehow he has developed this unity through centuries of adaptation to the desert's scorching heat and freezing cold. It

struck me that this harsh and unforgiving world was the anvil upon which the strongest of character was formed. Here was a beautiful way of life in which a man lived in harmony with his own existence. What more could happiness be?

Occasionally, we would meet a lone man in the desert with a small herd of camels or goats. Always, I found a great hospitality, a kindness of spirit that is absent in much of today's world. When I watched one man ride off alone on his camel, I wished that I could go with him. But that was his world. I could not go, yet in some ways I feel that I did . . .

VII

Throughout the Kingdom we found countless camels. Often the herds would be far on a distant horizon; other times we would have to maneuver among them in Jimmy. The camel is a constant landmark, from the rocky heights of the Asir mountains to the searing heat of the Empty Quarter. They seem always on the move in herds, searching for food and water in a dry, sparse land. The adaptability of the camel never ceased to amaze me.

On one occasion, I had climbed a slope of shale and rock. On reaching the crest, I again stood gazing across the hundreds of open miles that lay ahead. There was no wind, and all was silent except for a crackling noise. It sounded like someone breaking small sticks for a fire. I started down to investigate.

In a narrow *wadi*, several camels were munching peacefully on dry bushes. As always, they ignored my approach completely, and I walked within a few yards of them. To my surprise, they were feasting on a bush that made a barbed wire fence seem quite appetizing. Covered with three-inch thorns as sharp as needles, the branches of the bushes were being methodically ground up by the domino-sized teeth of the camels. Impossible though it seemed, the camels were quite content with their meal of thorns. I stood beside them watching them peacefully continue their afternoon snack. The only sound in the world was the intermittent crackle of the thorns and branches breaking in their powerful jaws . . .

His virtues and temperament aside, the camel is a major contributor to desert culture and heritage. Only with the camel were the great trade routes established to bring spices from the South. The camel provided the only means of transport for countless nomadic tribes of the desert, who migrated from area to area in search of food and water. The same "ship of the desert" enabled vast numbers of mighty warriors to cross nearly impenetrable areas and to build a modern nation.

During my journey, I have heard the camel described in every way imaginable: they were lazy, thoughtless, mean, vicious, unpredictable, stupid and useless. I also heard great tales of their immense strength, their incredible adaptability to the desert that allowed them to travel for days without water in searing heat and across terrain that would seem totally impassable. I met men who claimed to owe their lives to a camel.

Throughout the desert, great rocks and forms rise in mute testimony to the severe nature: wind and sand, heat and cold. Standing among such giants, I could only appreciate how small and frail I was in the shadow of the forces that mold the universe. . .

One evening, in the southern high desert between Najran and Abha, we spotted a lone camel moving quite methodically along a ridgeline in the distance. It was a sight I had seen countless times before, yet there was something in the steady walk of this camel that attracted my attention. I attached a telephoto lens to my camera to get a closer look. "There's a rider," I called to Kamal, who rolled his eyes heavenward. We had searched for someone actually riding a camel in the desert for so long that we began to consider it a myth. Actually, the sight of a camel and rider in the open desert has indeed become quite rare. "No—here, look at him," I said. "Look through the lens. There's a man riding the camel." I grew more excited as Kamal patiently looked through the long lens. I could scarcely believe our luck.

Kamal straightened. "You are right!" he said emphatically, and we both looked down at the rough rocks and sand between us and the disappearing rider.

"We must catch him," I said urgently. Kamal nodded. He always said we would find a camel and rider. Now with one in sight, the rough terrain between us gave the camel his due advantage. Nevertheless, we started off in Jimmy across the ragged ground, bouncing and bucking over the surface, leaving a plume of dust behind us. Everything in the truck clattered and bounced as we bucked our way toward the lone rider. I checked my compass and determined that we were heading north. I didn't want to repeat any of my past misjudgments.

Finally, we drew near the rider and stopped. With a few light flicks of his guide stick, the rider directed the camel beside us. The sight that followed was one that

Camel sequence: North of Najran

no one could forget. At a command and with some prodding from the rider, the camel began to fold and collapse his legs at various angles, gradually lowering and lurching his body to the ground, where he eventually settled in a neatly packaged bundle, his legs tucked beneath him. Amazing.

Kamal and Murieed went to talk with the rider, who stood almost at military attention. The camel rested behind him, his eyes half-closed. I changed films and lenses and went to meet our first camel rider. As usual, I could only communicate through my two friends. The man was extraordinarily polite, and he smiled at me with a nod after we shook hands and exchanged greetings.

We learned that he came from an encampment several miles north and was concerned to be on his way as evening was rapidly approaching. But our new acquaintance was very proud that we had come to see his camel, and he was determined to show him off at his best. He graciously offered us a ride, but I asked only that he would allow me to take several photographs of him on the camel. He found it difficult to understand why a strange, tall man from Hawaii wanted to photograph him on his camel, but he agreed with pleasure.

Anyone who has not seen a rider mount a camel has missed a unique event. After the proper amount of loud commands, a few well placed kicks and gestures from the rider, the camel literally springs from a peaceful, prone position. In a breath, camel and rider are suddenly thrust erect and propelled into forward motion, at a speed the human eye can scarcely perceive.

Our new friend had to depart. We followed for a mile or so, stopping so I could photograph from various angles. Then we waved and shouted farewell to him and headed south —by the compass —and arrived reassuringly back at the road, as the sun was settling on the mountains.

VIII

We found the village by accident. We were on a day trip investigating the mountains below Abha. It was a small village, about five miles from the highway to Al Yasid. There was nothing spectacular about it, but, since we were in no hurry, I decided to drive closer.

We stopped at the dry bed of a *wadi*, about a half-mile from the village walls. I got out of the car feeling rather strange. Something about the village seemed almost magical. I could see carefully-tended fields of bright-green barley, each neatly separated by two high walls of mud brick which formed a labyrinth of paths leading to the village. The architecture was typical of the southern mountains, and the buildings stood in neat rows, set close together. Each building, some five and six stories tall, was perfect—almost too perfect. It was as if the village came out of a storybook.

As I photographed, I became aware how neat and clean the village was. As a major resting point on the great trade routes, it must look now as it did centuries before. Caravans from Najran and Jizan had passed this very spot, then entered the narrow gates of the village to seek shelter and provisions, to trade. It all stood before me, as it had for centuries: a tribute to Arab heritage.

My imagination soared. I could visualize men walking in the narrow streets, small low shops beside the great buildings, camels at the wells. This magic village, like hundreds of similar villages, had been the center of a network of trade and commerce in the area. Beyond its fields and walls lay the vast open desert, where all was raw and barren. Through those open spaces with no boundaries or barriers roamed nomadic tribes and herdsmen. In that harsh environment, men learned to adapt to the land, to bend with the wind and recover—and to survive. They came to the village to trade, to rest. Some had stayed to raise crops and to develop a structured society, a different order and discipline.

Murieed broke the daydream with a touch of my arm. "Don't you want to go in?" he asked.

He startled me slightly. The way he phrased the question seemed symbolic: Didn't I want to go in?—as though there *was* only an "inside" or only an "outside." I began to sense the intimacy and warmth of the "inside" of Saudi culture—family, friendship, and hospitality—that was a protective barrier from the harsh environment, the empty spaces of the "outside."

We slid down the sand bank into the dry *wadi* and started across. The heat shimmered on the rocks; the sunlight seemed to vibrate in the air. It was one of the hottest days I had known. It was hot enough to burn the skin and the eyes, to dry and crack the lips, regardless of protection. It was a sun that had driven me under the traditional *ghotra*, which I draped over my head and wrapped around my chin and nose, leaving only a narrow slit for my eyes. Still, the sun would burn through it by the end of each day.

In the village, we walked between walled fields to the buildings. The narrow path between the walls opened into an outer courtyard before the buildings. Several elderly men greeted us from a side path. We stopped and shook hands. Murieed explained that I found their village quite beautiful, indeed one of the most beautiful I had seen in the Kingdom.

While they talked, I marvelled at the geometric order of the village: every corner and window was perfectly scaled and formed. It was impeccable. We stood talking in the sun. The men told Murieed that the village was over two hundred years old, and that their fathers and their fathers before them had all lived there. No, they had never thought of moving, either to the desert or to a larger city. They spoke proudly of their village and seemed quite pleased with our interest in it. I didn't want to disturb their day, however, so we merely asked if we could walk through the village.

They were happy to show us.

We set off on a lane between tall buildings. Each doorway was decorated with intricate geometric designs, with large forged rings and knobs. The village was quiet. The only signs of life were occasional glimpses of small children who gathered in a pathway or peered out from behind shutters. In some areas, the lane was so narrow that I felt as if I were at the bottom of a canyon of stone and mud brick. The sun seldom enters these lanes, and there is a wonderful dry coolness to the air.

At the rear of the village, toward the mountains, we arrived at a larger open square, backed by a huge fortress. One of the men went ahead and ducked into a doorway. I photographed the pathways and buildings while Murieed and Kamal talked with the others. I wanted to convey in photographs the peaceful, cool atmosphere of the village. Here there was no hustle and rush, all seemed amazingly ordered and tranquil.

The man returned from the fortress with a younger man, who he introduced as Tarik. After shaking hands, they left us with Tarik, who spoke very good English. He offered to show us his "farm," and we accepted.

We walked below a stone transom into a small pen, where the current flock of lambs rested quietly in the shade. Tarik explained that they were in the yard temporarily; soon they would be moved to the field with the entire flock. Meanwhile, by keeping them in the yard, they could herd them inside one of the rooms at night to avoid the cold.

This was my first visit to a true Arab fortress. We proceeded inside. It was dark and cool. It was an immense structure, at least six stories. Now it was used to store feed for animals and as an evening stall for the lambs. Still, it was magnificent. My imagination ran wild when I found vividly painted plaster walls in rooms with high, wood-beamed ceilings. On all sides, narrow slits revealed the surrounding terrain. Finally, after picking our way up the stairs in near darkness, we emerged breathless into the glaring sun of the flat roof.

Perspiring in the darkness, we had climbed several long flights of steps; and now we looked down on the entire village and surrounding fields. The view was spectacular. An exact line marked the edge of green fields—the

beginning of the desert. The roof afforded a clear view that stretched at least thirty miles in every direction.

Just staring across the dazzling sand brought visions of caravans descending the distant mountains, of warriors on horses and camels advancing on the village. The tightly grouped buildings provided a self-contained defense perimeter for the village.

When we reached the ground again, three men were resting patiently outside the door. We had no choice but to accept the invitation into their home for coffee and tea. Tarik explained that his father and uncle heard we were visiting the village and that they had prepared a small reception.

We entered the building and were shown to a carpeted side room, which had many large cushions against the walls. It was pleasantly cool in the darkened room. After leaving our shoes at the entrance, we had no difficulty making ourselves comfortable and stretching our toes. During the long coffee service, we told them of our project and travels. They found it curious that we had

decided to visit their village. Tarik's father said that it was "like many, many other villages," that there was "nothing special about it."

While they talked, I felt that we had returned to a past in which this magical village existed. We had seen no such villages; it was hardly typical. It was a perfect gem in itself. If anything, it was the classic Arab village of history, the most beautiful we had ever seen.

We lingered a long while over sweet tea in the cool room of whitewashed plaster. After we were finally able to leave and had walked back through the narrow passage-ways, I found a certain pleasure in the peaceful life of this village. For a short time we had been a part of it. We shook hands all around and again thanked Tarik for sharing some of his world with us. Only as we drove away did I look back and realize that we had never learned its name. I smiled to myself. I preferred to simply remember it as the perfect village . . .

IX

Though I marvelled at the villages and great castles, I was virtually astounded when we came upon lush green valleys, fields of crops, and cattle grazing on farms. I had never imagined such a vision in this land of deserts. Bright green squares of barley rippled in the breeze, sheltered by Ironwood windbreaks, planted by men who had tended these fields for generations. Behind the protective trees rose *Ad Dhana*, the giant dunes that are always restless, always moving. For centuries the Saudi has tended his flocks, tilled his soil, while the looming orange mountains shifted and crept silently about the desert. With a change of wind, flat, open areas could be invaded by the drifting sand that within weeks could form great soaring dunes, hundreds of feet high, and cover and obliterate all that was there.

East of Az Zilfi

Diriyah

Near Buraydah

I stood one day at the edge of a carefully-tended field. Rows of slender new shoots were waving in a slight breeze that blew across the cracked, dry earth. Beyond a row of trees, massive hills of sand towered like a huge wave above the valley floor, ready to flood across this delicately structured field before me. Each day the farmer would work the soil and look up at the great mountain of sand; he could not help but feel the staggering weight and mass that lay just beyond the trees. Yet some great inner confidence told him that all was well, and the farming continued year after year. Truly, some years not a drop of rain fell, and the sands blew with a fierceness that blinded his animals; yet he and his forefathers continued to work the soil and raise the crops. It was a harmonious yet fragile balance.

We visited farms that were hundreds of years old: some ran for miles along great valleys, some clustered near springs that flowed magically from the desert to fill intricate irrigation systems. Other farms were small and isolated, like miniature villages nestled unto themselves in rocky areas. These were completely self-contained, with high fortress structures and walls that enclosed the fields and animals. They usually stood alone in desolate areas, with only the emerald shimmer of crops and perhaps a solitary tree which attested to some hidden source of water.

My greatest amazement, however, was reserved for the herdsmen of this vast kingdom. During our many visits to the *Badu* encampments, I slowly came to know something of this traditional life in the open, although I could never fully comprehend the aptness of the herdsman. In the most arid and hostile terrain, he would quietly and peacefully lead his flocks by day and night. Some deep instinct was his guide, and he always seemed at peace with himself and the world.

One afternoon we were driving through a flat, hard desert, bright and barren like a dry lake bed. Through the shimmering heat and mirages, Murieed spotted something and we drove toward the elusive dark form. To my surprise, we drew up beside a herdsman and his flock of goats. Kamal approached and invited him to share our coffee, which we served in the shade beside the truck. Abu Karam said that he came from a camp to the east. I gazed across the sparkling white surface of the land and took a deep breath at the thought of crossing such an expanse with only a herd of goats for company.

We sipped the *gahwa*, and Abu Karam talked with Kamal in a most quiet voice. I can still hear his soft, gentle voice —the same voice he must have used to speak to his goats through the hot days and cold nights of solitude. While we rested and talked, the goats foraged about the floor of the desert, their heads lowered as they munched away at nearly invisible plants. How any living creature could find food out there was more than I could imagine.

Near Al Khamsin

Finally, we rose. Abu Karam walked a full circle around the flock, herded the goats into a group, and started them moving slowly northeast. We shook hands and exchanged farewells. As I said goodbye to him, I realized for the first time that he must have been older than I thought. His gentle voice and smiling eyes, however, radiated through the gray beard and weathered face. Regardless of his years, Abu Karam was still a young man . . .

X

It was an unusual evening. The sun was almost to the horizon, yet the heat weighed upon us like a moist hand. There was no wind. We had been wandering through Al Aflaj region in the truck, talking with farmers and pausing to explore some of the ancient fortresses that dotted the flat earth. Evening approached rapidly, and we pushed on toward the town of Layla in hope of finding a small hotel for the night.

Kamal was excited about something and was driving faster than usual. To my surprise, he scarcely slowed as we passed through Layla and headed south. Kamal had a determined smile on his face. "I know it's near here," he muttered. Before I could comment, he wheeled onto a dirt road and began weaving among the scrub brush.

"You're aware we just went through Layla?" I asked, trying not to betray my exhaustion.

"We'll return soon," Kamal said. "There is something you must see before sunset. Don't worry, we're almost there."

I glanced at Murieed to see if he was part of this private little plan, but he only rolled his eyes with a "here-we-go-again" expression. We swerved back and forth through the low brush, which stretched in every direction. From our past adventures, I knew we should stop soon for the night. As sunset approached, I finally asked: "How much longer, Kamal?"

"Any minute now," he laughed. "You won't believe what your eyes will see . . ."

I braced my feet on the dashboard wondering what could be so exciting to Kamal. It was all very mysterious. I was beginning to despair at the swaying and rolling of the truck on this strange pursuit. Just then, Kamal hit the brakes and we ground to a stop, and sat facing a low embankment of soft sand.

"Come!" he cried, setting off ahead of the truck. "We must hurry—soon it will be dark."

I swung the camera bag onto my shoulder and plodded after him. Murieed followed behind, bending to toss a pebble in boredom. We were all tired. However, as I reached the crest of the sand I awoke with a start.

Before us lay a large body of water. I blinked as though it were a mirage. The mirage remained, stretching almost a mile across. The crystal clear water fell off sharply from the sand into a silvery blue, then dark blue, then black. The surface was a mirror in the still air. When I put my hand into the water, small circles radiated out on the surface.

Truly, I did find it hard to believe my eyes. Here, alone in the desert, I felt we had discovered an unknown lake. Kamal obviously had been there many times, however. He took off his shoes, put his feet into the water and splashed happily. It was his treasure, his surprise — and he was going to enjoy every minute of it.

I made a number of photographs of this large lake in the sand, with its banks of reed-like grasses. The sun was low and I had little time to contemplate what I saw. I wanted to capture the solitude of this strange body of water surrounded by desert. It was immense and obviously quite deep; it gave a quality of peace and stillness to the evening desert.

Spring in Asir Mountains

"No, no," Kamal said, wagging his finger. We were now swerving back toward Layla in early twilight, with no idea of where we would spend the night. "No, it is *not* a lake," he repeated emphatically. "It is a spring!"

"How can there be such a spring out here?" I asked. "There isn't a rock or hill in fifty miles. It's all desert. It simply can't be a spring," I insisted. Whatever it was, it *was* there in the middle of Saudi Arabia, where I would never expect to see any water at all.

"I can prove it to you," Kamal said, arching his eyebrow. He waited for me to reply, his eyes twinkling.

"How?"

"There is no scientific evidence to prove or disprove it, but there is a very old story about this spring," he said seriously. "Many people have sworn to me that it is absolutely true, however."

We were almost back to the main road, but Kamal stopped the truck. He said that one day a group of people from Layla had come to picnic at the spring. It was something they did often because of the cool water. It seems that one of the families had a large Mercedes truck, and they had driven it to the spring that afternoon. No one is quite certain how it happened, and many have thought it was a prank played by some of the boys. . . Regardless, somehow the truck rolled slowly down the bank and plunged into the water. This, of course, caused a great uproar among everyone present.

The truck came to rest, its lonely cab looking like the bridge of a sunken ship. The people from the town rushed to the water. Several of the men splashed in and fastened one end of a rope to the bumper of the truck and the other to the rear end of a light pick-up truck. It was immediately apparent that it would take much more power to pull the giant truck from the water, so someone returned to Layla to get help.

Al Kharj

Soon a team of trucks and farm machines were also hitched with cables and ropes. After much roaring of engines and straining —even after a rope had been broken— the men had only rocked the truck back and forth, turning the water brown. If anything, it was deeper now and no closer to shore. To make the story short, Kamal said that finally there was nothing anyone could do. The truck was left in the spring, and everyone returned to town to devise a method of recovering it.

The next morning the people returned. The truck was gone! Some of the men dove into the water, which was again crystal clear, but found no trace of the vehicle. It had simply vanished! Kamal folded his hands in his lap and nodded his head with a smug expression. "Vanished," he repeated.

"And *that* proves it is a spring?" I asked with a frown.

"Wait, that is not all," he said. "The end of the story proves it is a spring."

For many weeks, people came from Layla to study the spring. No one ever found a trace of the truck. They went out in boats, but they never saw it again. For months this truck was the topic of conversation. Then gradually, people began to forget the vanished truck. Two years passed, then three. Finally no one spoke of the truck again.

Then one morning a man drove into Layla, his eyes wild with excitement. He jumped from his car and ran into the coffee house, shouting at the top of his voice. He was frantically searching for the man who lost his truck in the spring. The men in the coffee house calmed the man. He then told them that more than a year ago he left Layla to work in the oil fields. One afternoon he heard some workers from Al Hasa speaking of a large truck that they discovered sunken in the spring of an oasis near Hofuf. The workers said they were planning to use a huge "Caterpillar" to pull the truck out of the spring. The tale reminded the man of the truck in Layla, and he had driven over to see if they would succeed.

When he arrived, he nearly fainted at what he saw. The truck stood on the bank of the spring, water draining from every side. He gasped: It was the same truck! He ran around the wet monster and inspected it thoroughly. He wrote down the license plate, collected all the in-formation he could find from the vehicle, and drove through the night back to Layla.

It was the same truck, the same license number. Identical. Three years later and over three hundred miles away, this truck had surfaced in another spring from inside the earth.

"So, as you see," Kamal said, "since you know springs come from beneath the earth, this should prove to you that this is a spring."

I was speechless. Murieed began quizzing Kamal excitedly in Arabic. I could only sit and look back across the flat ground toward the moon, which was growing steadily brighter above the mysterious spring.

Because it was almost totally dark, we hastily arranged our gear and prepared to spend the night where we were. We worked in silence, each pondering the tale of the vanishing truck . . .

In the Kingdom, we visited many springs and oases, and walked the banks of many rivers and lakes, all of which seemed to belong to another world. However, none of them was so mysterious as the spring at Layla. . .

XI

Nowhere is the grandeur of Saudi Arabia's heritage more evident than in the silent stone sentinels that stand watch today over the peaceful desert. Once not long ago these castles and fortresses were the bastions of mighty warring tribes. Today thousands of watchtowers look across great valleys at each other, attacked now only by hawks, crows, and children.

In each city we visited stands at least one of these majestic structures, which usually dominates the highest points of land. Built of clay bricks or stones, they are hand-formed with a skill and precision that would dumbfound today's architects. The core of the structure is massive, heavily walled and fortified, and usually contains court-yards. Skilled craftsmen fortified them not with mortar or cement but with a precision of fitting that has allowed these fortresses to withstand mighty battles and cen-turies of wind and storm, cold, and heat.

These towers and castles fascinated me. Each mighty fortress held a special message to tell me and I strained to hear it speak. This was true of even the smallest watch-tower or walled farmhouse, and I tried to comprehend their silent words.

To Kamal's astonishment, I would often walk into the central courtyard of an abandoned fort and pace back and forth with my cameras in hand. I would study each doorway, arch, and detail. Eventually I would choose a place and sit down, sometimes for an hour or more, lost in thought. I had no visions or hallucinations. The only voices were the whispers and howls of the wind. Yet as I sat alone I would imagine men riding into the courtyard in flying robes. I could see the strain on a man's face as he would swing open the tall, wooden doors to allow a troop of men on camels to enter the walls.

There is an individual character to each mighty castle and fortress. The pride still lingers of the great men of the desert who strode these balconies and courtyards. I was endlessly turning at the sound of a whisper or a glimpse of a robe, finding only an Ironwood branch brushing against a plastered wall.

Within each of these great structures is the legend of legions of great men. Here lies the saga of their proud history and heritage. Here lies something great of the spirit of Saudi Arabia . . .

One afternoon in the mountains near Az Zafir, I climbed a hill to a rock watchtower. The day was bright and clear, with just a light wind blowing. Upon reaching the tower, I walked around it several times, as had become

my custom. On an impulse, I got to my knees and crawled through the square opening at the base. With only a slight effort, I lifted myself to a platform of bleached wood, and then climbed to the rim of the tower and sat on the ledge.

Kamal and Murieed were far below me, having tea beside Jimmy. I knew they found my interest in the towers rather strange; and they had decided to watch from a distance by that time, rather than follow me up and down every tower and fortress we discovered.

I sat alone in the tower and watched the valley below me. After some time, a history began to unfold. It was fascinating. First, I heard a scraping noise. Although it sounded nearby, the scraping came from far across the valley: a man bending over his work. He appeared to be digging little trenches to plant seeds in the terraced land. Then a flock of sheep appeared on the distant hillside. They moved like a gray-white cloud over the land, followed by a shepherd in a white *thaub*. I felt quite at home and comfortable watching the activity below me.

It is wonderful to be alone with your thoughts in such a vast land. Here was complete solitude, a solitude that brought a sense of freedom. I watched the valley with an almost hypnotic gaze, as much at peace as the grazing sheep. Finally the spell faded. I carefully picked my way back down the tower and crawled through the opening.

As I rose to my feet, I was jolted back to reality: not ten feet away, an old man was sitting on a stone wall. He must have been watching me all the time. I felt awkward but greeted him in Arabic. He politely returned the greeting, after rising with a slight bow. Thoughts raced through my head: I wondered if it was his land, his tower. Somehow I never had considered that the towers might be "owned" by anyone.

The man took a step toward me and said something in Arabic. His voice was even, as emotionless as his face. I smiled and tried to appear friendly. I said in English that I had been up in the tower watching the valley. As a gesture of satisfaction, I patted the tower with my free hand.

The old man smiled, walked over to the tower, and looked up and down at it. He nodded his head and patted the stones very gently, almost affectionately. He then stepped back several paces and scratched his head, still looking at the tower. Again he smiled. I wondered if we both heard voices from the stones.

He looked across the valley with a peaceful expression. He wore the traditional *thaub*, another heavier robe, and the red-and-white checked *ghotra*, which he draped loosely over his head, much as I did. At his belt was a beautiful dagger and scabbard of silver filigree. He swept his arm into the air and said something I didn't understand, then looked at me as though waiting for a reply. Using the few Arabic words I knew, I said that I couldn't speak Arabic, hoping he would understand me. He only shook his head. He squinted at me and looked displeased. I glanced at the road, about a quarter-mile downhill. No sign of my two companions. I was alone with this old man who seemed determined to tell me something. He

paced over to the wall surrounding the tower and pointed to the far slope. He made a motion with his hand as though a flight of birds were skimming down the hillside. I walked over and tried to see what he was showing me, but was met by only the silent wind.

For some time we stood looking across the valley. The old man rubbed his chin, and he seemed to be watching something. It occurred to me that he made a perfect photographic subject. I wanted to explain this, for I didn't want to photograph him without his permission. But how?

I asked in English if I could photograph him, and gestured with the camera toward the tower. Facing me directly, he stared at me intently but gave no sign of understanding.

I pretended to "position" the tower with my hands. Then I backed up, pointed the camera at it, released the shutter, and nodded with a smile. I then went over to the man and made the same positioning gestures, backed up, and pretended to take his picture with my empty hands. The old man laughed. I felt like an idiot.

Abha Fortress

Then he waved an upturned palm toward the sky and turned back to the valley. I got the impression that he didn't mind and was signalling me to go ahead and photograph. I walked off to the side and focused the camera on him. He paid no attention at all, so I exposed several frames. He seemed far away in thought, and there appeared no way to "pose" him. I made another photograph and thanked him in Arabic. He looked up with a puzzled expression. I smiled, shook his hand, and motioned that I had to leave. I swung the camera over my shoulder, smiled, and thanked him again as I turned toward the tower.

A scream split the air!

I whirled around. The old man was waving his huge knife over his head. It gleamed in the sunlight. I stepped back.

He was crying out a shrill chant and hopping from one foot to another in a steady rhythm. He brandished the mighty knife back and forth and watched me with flashing eyes.

Instinctively, I made a quick photograph of the old man leaping about with his knife, at the same instant thinking I was crazy to do it. He might kill me!

I backed cautiously toward the tower, my eyes fixed on the long blade of the dagger. His eyes were glazed, and he called out strange sounds as he bobbed back and forth.

My heart was pounding and my mouth was suddenly dry.

I stood transfixed, unable to take my eyes from him. Desperately, I thought how I could protect myself from the knife if he came for me. He didn't move toward me; nor did he stop his rhythmic jumping from foot to foot, calling out under his breath. Where was Kamal?

Then he stopped. Carefully, he put the blade back into the scabbard. He looked up just as a howl of laughter burst from behind the tower. Murieed and Kamal stumbled into view, both doubled over with laughter and clutching at each other to keep their feet. Slowly, I began to understand.

They had tricked me again . . .

It turned out they had met the old man on the road and told him of their strange friend in the tower. He too had found it amusing and agreed to pay me a visit. He told them he would do one of the old tribal victory dances to surprise me. He had certainly succeeded.

XII

Nowhere is the division of land and sea more dramatic than in Saudi Arabia. Shimmering blue water stretches to one horizon, and shimmering sand desert to the other. The two elements are so totally different that their junction defies the logic of the eye. Yet, desert and sea have much in common.

For centuries, a special breed of nomad has roamed the seas. His world is not one of sand and mountain; it is one of raging storms, of calm windless days, of tides and currents, and of endless shifting waves. He is the fisherman. The fish of the seas form his flock. Each day he searches the vast waters of the Gulf or Red Sea to bring in his catch. He too must adapt to his own harsh desert.

We had driven north to Qatif only to find the fishing fleet at sea. I stood on the empty dock looking seaward, a damp, warm breeze in my face. I made several photographs of the few boats that bobbed listlessly beside the pier. Far at sea, the great Arab fishing boats were at work.

I noticed several boats further north, just offshore, and pointed them out to Kamal. He studied them for some time through my long telephoto lens. "Those are the boats. They must be off Tarut Island," he said after some reflection.

Qatif

"Let's visit them," I said quickly. Thus began another day in our search for the *Badu* of the sea. We'd driven far: Qatif, Jubayl, Tarut, Jedda, Jizan. But since Jimmy could not swim, we could only find these proud fishermen when they returned to the edge of their desert —to our shoreline.

Tarut is an island on the map, a fishing village through history. Today a fine roadway bridges the mile of water; and crossing over it we shortly found ourselves in town. We drove slowly into the crowd. It was market day: the *souk*. Everyone from miles around milled beneath the canvas awnings of the bazaar. Bargains were sought for everything from fish and vegetables to beautiful hand-woven baskets. Men shouted to each other, leading goats and sheep down narrow streets, carrying birds and chickens in cages. Three children ran a lemonade stand on one corner of the *souk*. With absolute charm they handed out glasses of refreshment to the shoppers.

After winding Jimmy around dozens of narrow corners, we at last arrived at the Gulf. Several small rowboats were tied offshore, and far beyond the shallow water, a fleet of the classic Arab fishing boats rode at anchor. After the excitement of the *souk*, the shoreline was remarkably peaceful. The smell of salt air and fish drifted in from tiny waves that washed at the sand. The waterfront was deserted, except for three men sitting in the shade of a low building.

Qatif

We walked over and Murieed asked them if it was possible to visit the fishing boats. As always, we wound up explaining our entire project to a fascinated audience, then joining them inside for coffee. They said it would be possible to visit the boats, but the crews were all at the *souk*. Perhaps if we only wanted a closer look to photograph them, they could help us.

One of the men hiked up his *thaub* and waded into the water until it was almost up to his knees. "*Yallah,*" he called back to us, "Let's go."

I looked at the distance to the nearest rowboat, then back at Kamal. "It's up to you, my friend," he said, pretending to untie his shoe.

"Why not?" I thought. I sat down, pulled off my shoes and rolled my trousers above my knees. This seemed the only way to get nearer the boats; so disregarding the prospect of a long wade, we went splashing through the warm water after the man.

When we reached the rowboat, we had waded several hundred yards. Although it was anchored, the rowboat was also aground on shallow tidal flats. Thus, after I put my camera case into the stern, we pushed the boat, half floating, half scraping, toward deeper water. At last it was afloat. Murieed climbed in first and Kamal was on

Khamis Mushayt

134

Jizan

the gunnel, when it became obvious that the boat was once again aground. Nothing is simple. So, out they climbed, and we again pushed the boat seaward.

So it went until finally we had pushed the boat almost half a mile offshore. We were wet to the waist by the time we could all climb into the boat. Abdullah, our new leader, took this in stride, as he cheerfully sculled with one oar to the fishing boats.

Jizan

As we moved among the boats, I made many photographs. These hulls had evolved through centuries of Arab seagoing history. Their design had been refined and adapted to become what lay before us now: a totally functional ship, able to sail any waters with crew and cargo. The hulls offered a wealth of photographic design studies. We kept Abdullah sculling for almost an hour, until my film supply ran low. He seemed to enjoy our little cruise. His forehead was beaded with perspiration, however, and I told him how much we appreciated his kindness.

Our return was like the departure —with one exception. The tide had fallen and we ran aground even further offshore. We tried to thank Abdullah by towing him in the boat as far as possible. He would not hear of it! He jumped in after us, and together we pulled the rowboat to the shallows, anchored it, and waded ashore.

After more coffee and much laughter about our exercise, we bid Abdullah and the others farewell and started back down the coastline. We returned to Qatif harbor — just in case any of the boats had returned.

Jedda

137

Jubayl

Qatif

Incredible luck: a large fishing boat with its decks filled with fish was rounding the breakwater, heading for the dock. At last, I could get some photographs of a working boat at sea, plowing its way through the water. Excitedly, I took out the cameras and worked furiously while the crew brought the boat in and started to unload its cargo. Seldom had our timing been so opportune.

The crew was cheerful, and invited us aboard the boat, which was sturdy and well built, perfect for its work. I photographed until I was afraid we were hindering the crew, who had been at sea for five days. Once again, after

many thanks and farewells, we headed north to Jubayl. Before sunset, we had revisited all the ports along a hundred miles of coast, and had gotten to know many friendly and helpful men of the fishing fleets.

In Jedda and Jizan, we were treated to Red Sea craftsmanship. The boat builders in Jizan still follow the tradition of forming each hull by hand. Yet, they took time to show us the method of their craft and the precision of the results. Several crews invited us to sail with them. Tempting though it was, I felt that we should continue our journey.

Kamal and Murieed actually seemed eager to continue. This seemed odd for usually they were the ones who wanted to stay longer. Then it came to me. Weeks before, I had told them that I had been in the Navy and loved the sea. Kamal had mentioned his seagoing experience: *both he and Murieed got seasick!*

To my delight, I had remembered. As we climbed into Jimmy, I decided this was the perfect time to repay some of their many pranks and jokes.

"Kamal," I began, trying to sound thoughtful.

"Yes, what is it?"

I shrugged my shoulders: "You know, I've been thinking. You're right. We always rush from place to place. I think we should spend more time with the same people and really get to know them. Do you remember Ali's offer to sail to Jedda? Perhaps we should go with him tomorrow."

A rare silence filled the truck. Kamal said something to Murieed in Arabic. He had not yet started the engine.

"This is too good an opportunity to miss, don't you agree?" I asked, putting several lenses into a case, as though packing for a long voyage.

Jizan

There was a long pause . . .

". . . Do you wish to sail with them to Jedda?" Kamal asked.

"Of course; then we all return with the boat to Jizan next week, pick up the truck, and continue," I added, to avoid any suggestion of them driving the truck to Jedda to meet me.

Another silence.

Kamal glanced down at the map. "If we go, we may not have time for much of the coast you wanted to see," he said.

"But don't you think it might be even more interesting to do some photographs of the coastal towns from the water? We might even stop at an island—you mentioned there were islands off the coast," I said with renewed enthusiasm.

Kamal looked around at Murieed, then back at me, and sighed a deep breath. "Well . . . if that is your wish . . ." he said, with a trailing voice.

I laughed and slapped the dashboard. I couldn't continue it further. "I'm joking," I said with a grin. "We really don't have the time, although it would be a good trip."

"I think you're right, my friend," Kamal said, quickly starting the engine. "We have too many wonderful things to see."

I could almost feel the sighs of relief as we turned back onto the roadway . . .

XIII

I shuddered in the thin, cold air and stamped my feet.
I was freezing. We had driven on a side road to a lookout
high in the Asir mountains, south of Taif. The view
across the mountains to the Red Sea was spectacular. On
all sides, small birds chirped and flitted from the
branches of pine trees; and Arabian crows and hawks
wheeled majestically on air currents above the cliffs.

Cliffs below Taif

At six thousand feet, the air was thin and chill. It was a
totally different world from the desert below. Kamal
had driven us to the lookout in late afternoon, then
taken the truck back to the last village to rest in a coffee
house. Now Murieed and I stood on the rock ledge,
patiently watching the sun settle silently into the haze.
We rubbed our arms to keep away the chill. The
cameras were ready on tripods; and every few minutes
I made several photographs, feeling better at least to
record the slow descent of the sun.

Some of the finest sunsets in the world occur in Saudi Arabia, and that night it was magnificent. With cold, stiff fingers, I quickly made many exposures as the sun reached the horizon. It was the most peaceful of sunsets: the last glowing ember winked below the Red Sea, leaving the world bathed in a blue and purple light.

I hurriedly folded the tripods, as darkness was rapidly settling upon us. I knew Murieed was even colder than I for he wore only a light vest over his *thaub*. He helped me put the cameras and lenses in their cases with great eagerness, and suggested we walk back to the side road to meet Kamal. We carefully picked our way over the large rocks, balancing with tripods and camera cases. Soon we were stumbling along the darkened trail to the road.

Finally, I had begun to appreciate the vast distances in the Kingdom. Then, looking in both directions, I again became aware of their magnitude as we stood beside the deserted road. Emptiness.

The metal tripod was so cold that I placed it on the ground beside the cases, then jammed my hands into my pockets. "I hope he doesn't forget us," I said, pressing my arms to my sides.

Murieed merely shuffled his feet in the dust and then hopped up and down on both feet like a bird. How could it be this cold? I had no idea of the temperature, but in such dry air, I suspected it was colder than it felt. "Maybe we should walk along the road to warm up," I said.

"It's better that we wait here, I think. We don't want to miss Kamal," he replied.

Then it dawned on me: although we were in no danger, standing there in the cold, once again we were essentially lost. I knew only that it was about ten miles back to the last village on the side road. From there it must have been sixty miles to Taif on the highway. But Kamal should arrive any minute, and we would warm up in Jimmy on the way back to town.

The moon rose over the ridge, and a bluish light outlined every rock and tree—and the empty road. The moonlight brought on something of a hypnotic trance. My mind began to drift and I dreamed of many things far away in the past. I gazed sleepily at the distant ridge and wondered what men had first travelled these mountain tracks and made the great trade routes. In the silence, I could somehow envision the great caravans bringing frankincense from the South. But now there were no caravans; they lived on only in spirit and my imagination.

Where was Kamal?

The moon was higher now. Murieed and I had been deep in our separate thoughts as we paced back and forth. I wondered if something had possibly happened to our friend. At such moments, the mind imagines a thousand things: Maybe the truck broke down; maybe he couldn't find the small road in the dark. The possibilities tumbled endlessly. For the moment it meant only that we might have to walk to the village. Perhaps we would meet a vehicle, although it seemed unlikely on this road. No matter. I stamped my feet in the dust and returned to my dreams of caravans.

Then, standing half-frozen in the moonlight, I realized we had been tracing the historic trade routes of the ancient Arab world. Along these roads we had seen and visited a myriad of castles and villages, farms and towers. The endless watchtowers and fortresses that lay along our route had witnessed the legacies of history. Today they stood as silent monuments to the grandeur of Saudi heritage . . .

My dreams were interrupted by the rattle of an approaching vehicle. Through the brush we could see headlights bobbing up and down. This apparition turned into our beloved Jimmy. Kamal brought him to a stop and we piled equipment into the back and jumped into our seats. Greeted by the warm air in the truck—the heater was going full blast—I realized how cold it was outside. I rubbed my hands together and took a deep breath.

"Sorry, gentlemen," Kamal said, leaning forward on the steering wheel.

Only then did we learn how fortunate we were not to have to walk back to the village. Kamal had taken a wrong turn, and he too had watched the sunset, but from another ridge north of us. Finally, he had made his way back and found the correct road in the dark. Clearly, he had been worried, but I assured him that we were quite alright. Even Murieed agreed, as he handed us cups of hot coffee from the thermos with hands that were still trembling from the cold.

We drove in silence for almost an hour, watching the moonlight and shadows skim across the land. I was deep in thought, my forehead leaning against the window. So many visions had come to me in this land, so much had stirred my imagination.